Riffs, Licks & Tricks
you can learn today!

FastForward™

Rock 'n' Roll
Piano

with Bill Worrall

HAL•LEONARD®

Published by
Hal Leonard

Exclusive distributors:
Hal Leonard
7777 West Bluemound Road, Milwaukee, WI 53213
Email: info@halleonard.com

Hal Leonard Europe Limited
42 Wigmore Street Marylebone, London, WlU 2 RY
Email: info@halleonardeurope.com

Hal Leonard Australia Pty. Ltd.
4 Lentara Court Cheltenham, Victoria 9132, Australia
Email: info@halleonard.com.au

Order No. AM963700
ISBN 0-7119-8129-9
This book © Copyright 2001 Hal Leonard

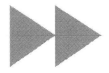

Written and arranged by Bill Worrall.
Music processed by Paul Ewers Music Design.
Edited by Sorcha Armstrong.
Picture research by Nikki Lloyd.
Artist photographs courtesy LFI / Redferns.

Printed in the EU

www.halleonard.com

Introduction

Hello, and welcome to ▶▶Fast*Forward*.

Congratulations on purchasing a product that will improve your playing and provide you with hours of pleasure. All the music in this book has been specially created by professional musicians to give you maximum value and enjoyment.

If you already know how to 'drive' your instrument, but you'd like to do a little customising, you've pulled in at the right place. We'll put you on the fast track to playing the kinds of riffs and patterns that today's professionals rely on. We'll provide you with a vocabulary of chord sequences and Rock 'n' Roll riffs that you can apply in a wide variety of musical situations, with a special emphasis on giving you the techniques that will help you in a band situation.

▶▶Fast*Forward* *Rock 'n' Roll Piano* is an amazingly infectious piano style that we'll be explaining to you from basics to advanced techniques to show you how to become an authentic foot-stomping Rock 'n' Roll pianist!

You'll be learning the secrets of Rock 'n' Roll legends such as **Little Richard**, **Ray Charles**, **Fats Domino**, and **Jerry Lee Lewis**, and we'll also give you a host of other tips for authentic Rock 'n' Roll playing. If you've been playing for about 6 months to a year, can play comfortably with both hands together, and are familiar with some scales and chords, this is the book that will take you further. If you're a beginner or new to the piano, I recommend that you try a beginners method such as *Absolute Beginners Keyboard* or *The Complete Piano Player* (details on page 64) before moving on to this book.

All the music examples in this book come with full-band audio tracks so that you get your chance to join in. Practise and learn the examples and then take off on your own over the backing tracks!

All players and bands get their sounds and styles by drawing on the same basic building blocks. With ▶▶Fast*Forward* you'll quickly learn these, and then be ready to use them to create your own style.

Rock 'n' Roll

How did it happen and where did it come from?

Culturally, it was a simple mixture of two things, Black and White; musically a marriage of Rhythm and Blues and country (and city money). R & B, socially, came about for similar reasons to Rock 'n' Roll a decade or more earlier. It started with the migration of blacks from the South who were desperate to escape racism and to improve their standard of living. They headed for northern cities like Chicago whose population of 50,000 increased five times in the period between the wars. For many there was a stigma attached to the countrified blues of the South and they sought an urban and harder edged music of their own.

An important contributor in forging this new style was the recent arrival of the electric guitar. Two of the biggest names were **Howlin' Wolf** and Chuck Berry's idol **Muddy Waters**. Their music, though increasingly popular (as confirmed by the introduction of Billboard's R & B charts at the end of the 1940s), was still excluded from white radio stations. White artists, aware of its commercial potential, were already recording 'lyrically sanitised' versions of 'prurient' R & B songs.

Come the fifties, for literally the first time in history (particularly for whites), there was a generation of youngsters with money to spend, who wanted their own music and heroes. For astute D.J. **Alan Freed**, Rock 'n' Roll was a commercial euphemism for R & B enabling him to foster corporate sponsorship and reach a wider audience. **Bill Haley** was already pushing 30 when 'Rock Around The Clock' started the ball rolling although he never had the voice of **Little Richard**, **Ray Charles**, or **Elvis Presley**. White teenagers now had their own hero and the rest, as they say, is history.

In keeping with most types of music, the piano in Rock 'n' Roll is performing one of two roles, either accompanying or soloing (which includes playing the tune or improvised soloing). In this book the material has been divided between these two activities. In music, as in life (and certainly in Rock 'n' Roll piano), the accompanying role isn't always glamorous. But while some of the parts may not always feel enormously interesting, it's crucial for a band to have a good 'rhythm' section and underlying groove.

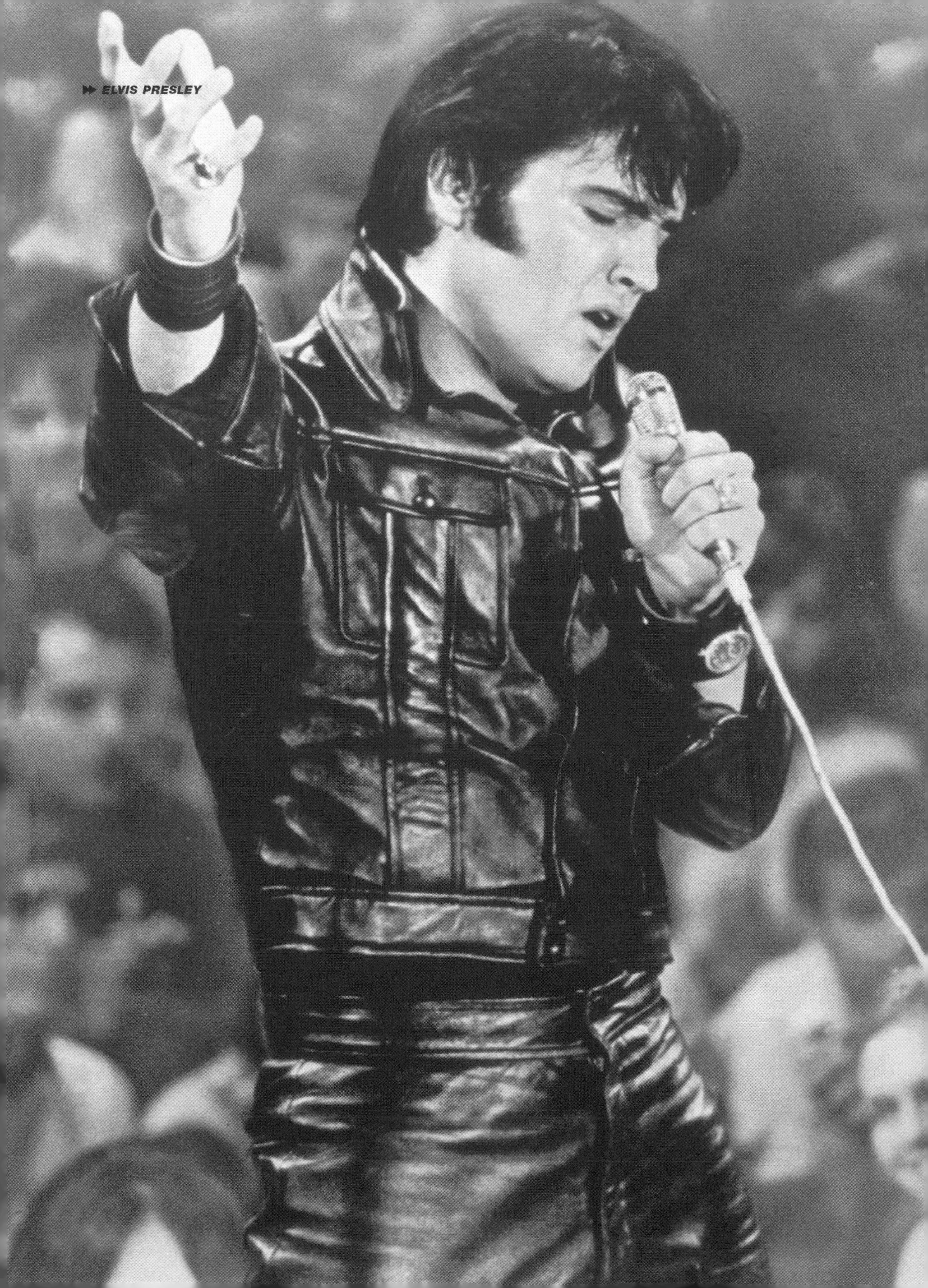

Chapter 1: Piste Again

Jer-Gah-Gah

I've always found that a very useful way to convey musical ideas and phrasing, (for any instrument) is to sing the line in some form. If you've ever listened to the music of Sir Thomas Beecham or Herbert Von Karajan, you may be familiar with the odd 'Pom-Pom' or 'La-La' – but these are a bit tame for this opus of inebriation! When the time comes to teach the rest of your band your right hand phrasing, you'll know what to sing!

Whether or not you decide to sing Jer - Gah - Gah in time with your right hand, with or without this phonetic aid, you should breeze through this example. Simple though it is, you only need to add another 'gah' to your right hand on beat three and you're playing the piano part to multi-million seller 'Will You Still Love Me Tomorrow'.

TRACKS 1+2

Jer-Ger Jer-Ger

If you are like most right handed pianists, you might find your left hand is not quite as agile as its opposite number. So, for those of you still in need of some gentle cosseting, this example gives the illusion of the left hand doing more than is actually the case. You could also try singing Jer - Ger - Jer - Ger in quavers along with the left hand part for an authentic Rock 'n' Roll sound.

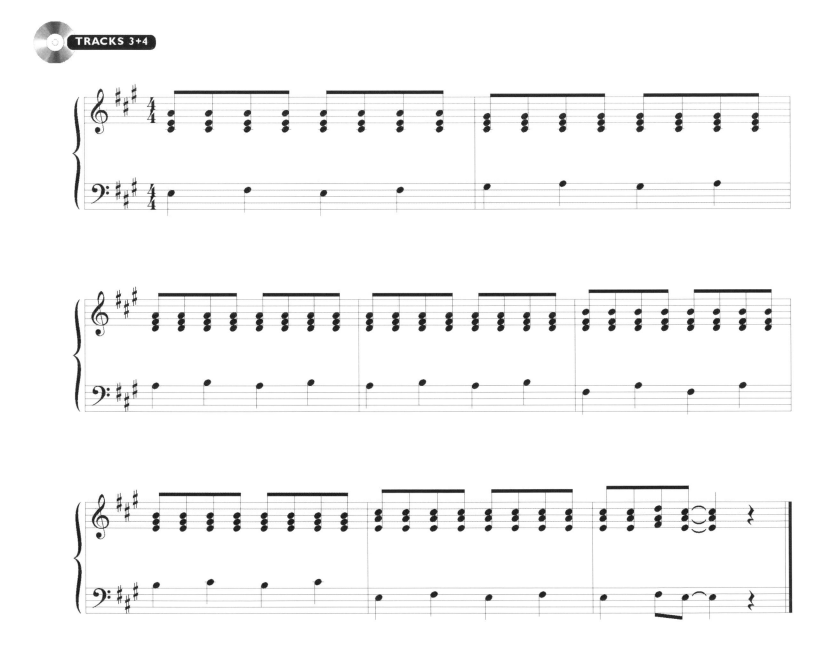

TRACKS 3+4

Bid-al-e-Bum Bur-Dah

Unlike many tortuous tongue twisters, this one
literally slides off your lips and, being reminiscent
of the 'Spanish triplets' in 'Baby Stay' you should
find it gives it a subtle rhythmic twist. **Elton
John** didn't harm his bank balance using this
idea on 'Crocodile Rock'.

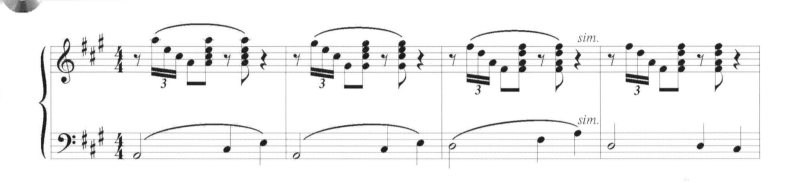

Bup Bur-Dah

Well you should, by now, be well and truly at
ease with this phonetic approach, but the left
hand has more of a work-out on this occasion,
having to play what it managed surreptitiously to
avoid on page 10. This example also
demonstrates one approach to using the root +
fifth, to root + sixth left hand pattern, on chords
other than the usual ones of I, IV and V (in this
case the mediant III in bar 2 and the supertonic
II in bar 5). Why not do some experimenting?

TRACKS 7+8

PAY LESS AT
ERRY LEE LEWI
MUSIC TRUCK
CORDS AT WHOLESALE... OR NEARL

Shout

We've looked at elements of the Twist and now it's time to Shout and have some Latin fun. I've opened with a rhythmically fragmented figure, which establishes a mood and sets up the piece. You can find similar examples in tracks as diverse as **Eddie Cochran**'s 'Summer Time Blues' and

'Nut Rocker' by **Bee Bumble and the Stingers**. The second half of this tune has a more Latin flavour to the piano part and feels very different from the opening twist sections of this chapter. Notice how the same 'twist' drums part works for both styles.

TRACKS 9+10

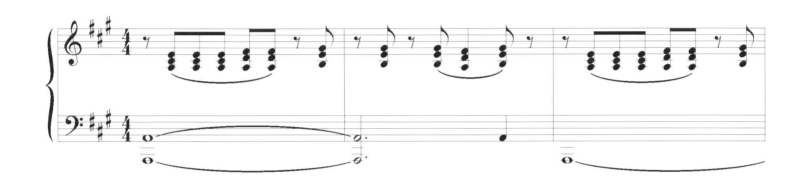

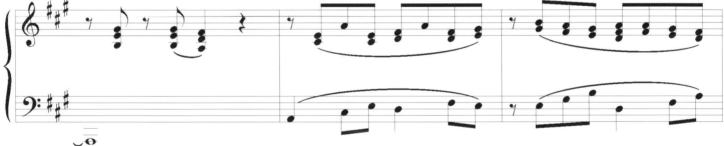

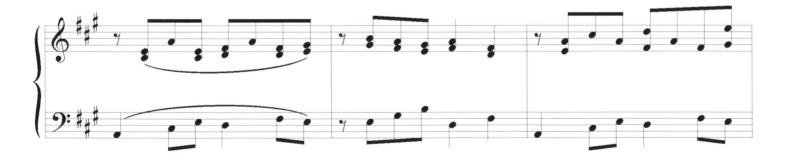

Piste and Shout

Improvisations have a notorious habit of looking messy and unfriendly on the page, here's an example of a typical improvisation. The piece is fairly busy as there are lots of different ideas for you to experiment with. You can use any of these are a starting point for your own improvisations. Here's what to look out for:

- Bars 1 & 2: an opening fanfare tremolando followed by gliss.
- Bars 3 & 4: the 'Chuck Berry riff' followed by

a descending touch of 'Floyd Cramer'.
- Bars 5 & 6: a variation of the previous (page 13) Latin figure.
- Bars 7 & 8: crotchet triplets with a pedal A at the top.
- Bars 9 & 10: off-beat quaver brass type line, followed by an arpeggiated triplet quaver pattern.
- Bars 12 & 13: ascending pentatonic octave figure concluding with forte tremolando.

TRACKS 11+12

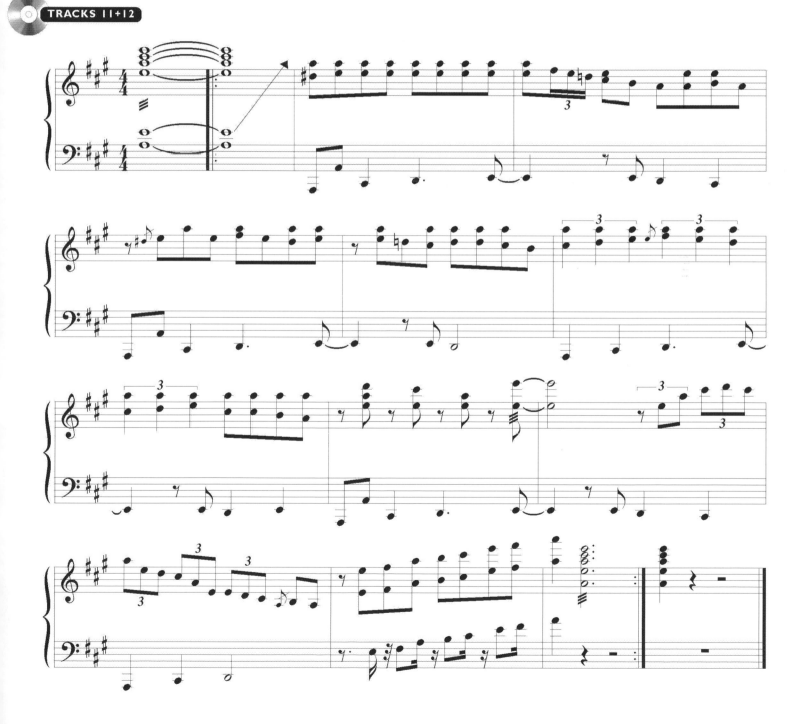

Chapter 2: Baby Stay

Fifth Chords

One of the most common features of Rock 'n' Roll piano is the repeated chord, mainly because in a band situation, it was the only way for the piano to be heard. Sometimes these are played as a complete chord and often (particularly in the higher register) as 'fifth' chords (root and fifth only). They are frequently accompanied by a sharpened 4th or flattened 5th at the start of a group of 3 or 4 quavers. Another useful device, which is often found with the repeated chord pattern, is accenting notes in groups of three. This type of rhythm is often used with four groups of three followed by one group of four (or two groups of two), as shown below.

TRACKS 13+14

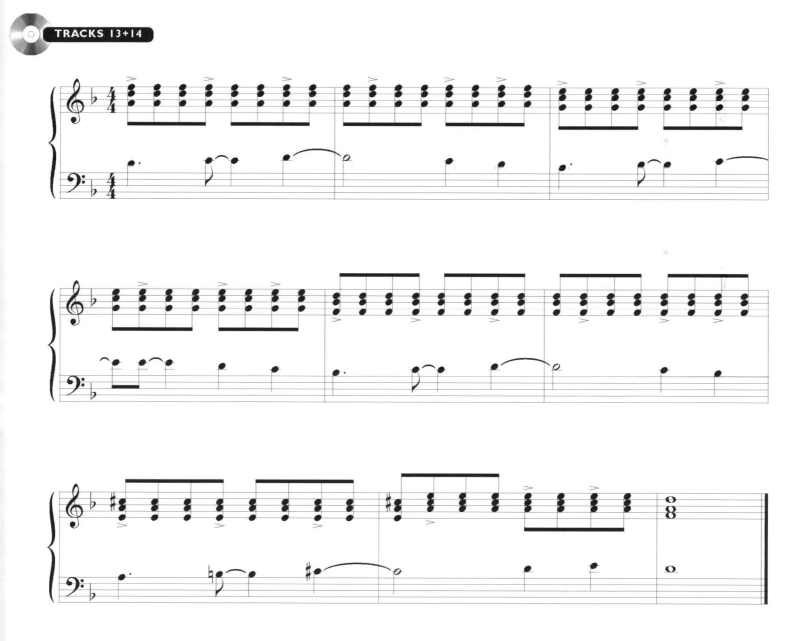

Thirds

If you're lucky enough to have a sensitive band to play with, then you should be able to take the tune every now and then. Your single line might be improved by adding thirds to it. This example happens to work pretty well using thirds throughout, but don't assume that simply adding another third on top is the magic solution; harmony's not always that simple. If you really need to strengthen it, one way is to double the melody line down the octave (i.e. add the note an octave below to each note of the melody line).

TRACKS 15+16

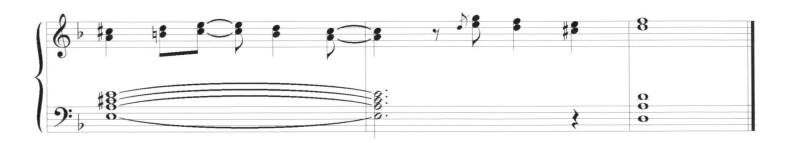

8s Figure

Here, I've created a right hand figure which has a
nice mixture of harmonic and melodic elements.
So, you end up with a part which fulfils its
harmonic role but also, because of the melodic
contours, provides melodic and rhythmic interest.
With Rock 'n' Roll piano, this is really what you
should be aiming for as much as possible.

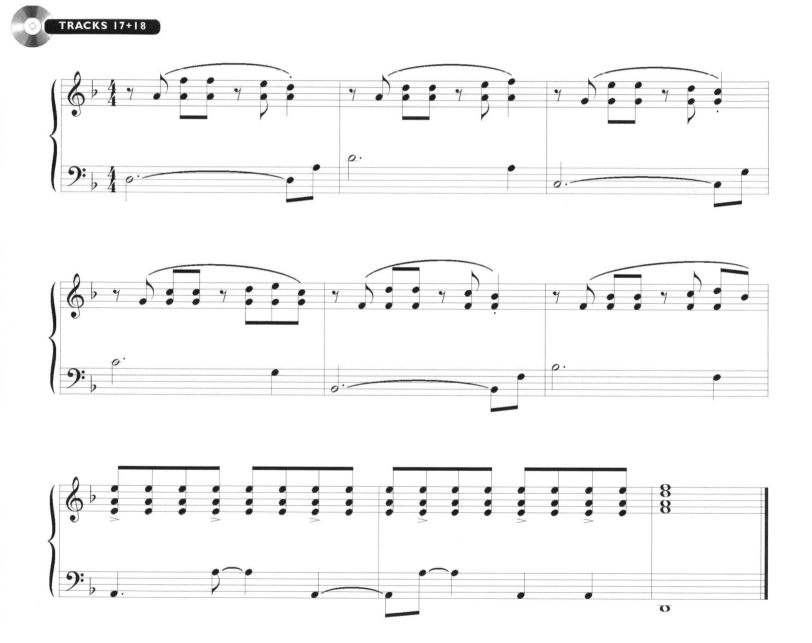

TRACKS 17+18

The Spanish Connection

There's something about this arpeggiated triplet figure that invariably makes me think of Spain. To hear it in action, check out **Del Shannon**'s first release 'Runaway' which topped both the U.K. and U.S. charts in 1960. Apart from being a great song it's also interesting for the unique 'Musitron' solo which influenced fashionable synthesiser 'noodlings'* of later decades.

TIP

*To Noodle: pianists' tendency to wander aimlessly but with great purpose over the tune. Characterised by occasional brilliance but more commonly long, boring and repetitious.

TRACKS 19+20

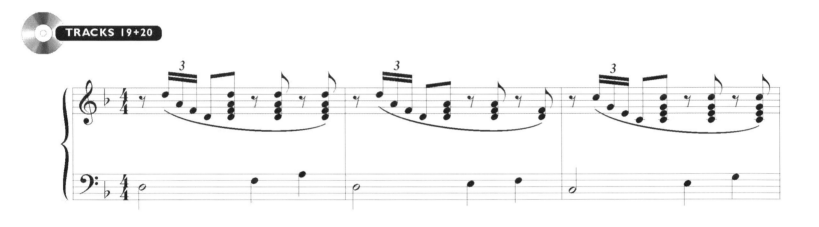

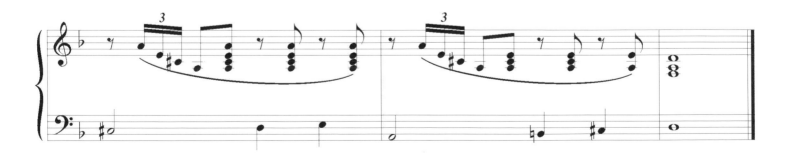

Octave Tune

This final piece is a double length version of previous examples, and features the tune played in octaves. Here, the left and right hands are playing in unison, but there is also a separate left hand part if you'd like to play alone (i.e. without the CD or a band). Using unison octaves is

another useful device which enables the piano to cut through the sound of a band when a single line might not be loud enough. You could also try this two octaves apart or an octave or two down for some interesting changes in colour.

Chapter 3: Strawberry Pill

Although Rock 'n' Roll might seem to be characterised by high-energy, frenzied performances, there's one man for whom the term 'laid-back' might have been invented. He had over sixty singles in Billboard's R & B charts and was a major player in Rock 'n' Roll piano. He is of course 'Mr. Casual' – **Fats Domino**, (born in New Orleans in 1928). He was already a chart success prior to the 1955 Rock 'n' Roll era and one of his many successes was 'Blueberry Hill'. Regrettably he's been stubbornly reluctant to record my own obvious follow up, 'Strawberry Pill', but to redress the balance I'm going to use it for the following example. This is the slowest piece in this collection, which I have written in triplets in 4/4 rather than in 12/8.

▶▶ FATS DOMINO

Repeated Chords

Apart from the roll in bar 2 the right hand part is all about repeated chords, which we'll see is one of the mainstays of Rock 'n' Roll piano. Despite this repetition and seeming simplicity, it is still desirable to have some form of shape and direction for the piece. One good way to do this is to imagine how you would phrase it if you were playing an instrument such as a saxophone or trumpet. Possibly the best practice of all is simply to sing it. Rock 'n' Roll is full of nonsense lyrics, so just find something phonetic that fits the rhythm and helps give those potentially tedious repeated chords some life of their own. The bass line, as in other examples, is another simple but classic figure that's based on an arpeggio of a major triad.

Right Hand Bounce

The right hand figure is yet another of those timeless riffs which, along with its variations (which we'll explore in other examples), has probably sold more records than all other riffs put together. This is the sort of line that 'Fats' really made his own and to do justice to his style it should sound as effortless as possible. To achieve this, keep your wrist completely loose, and let the chords simply 'bounce' off each other.

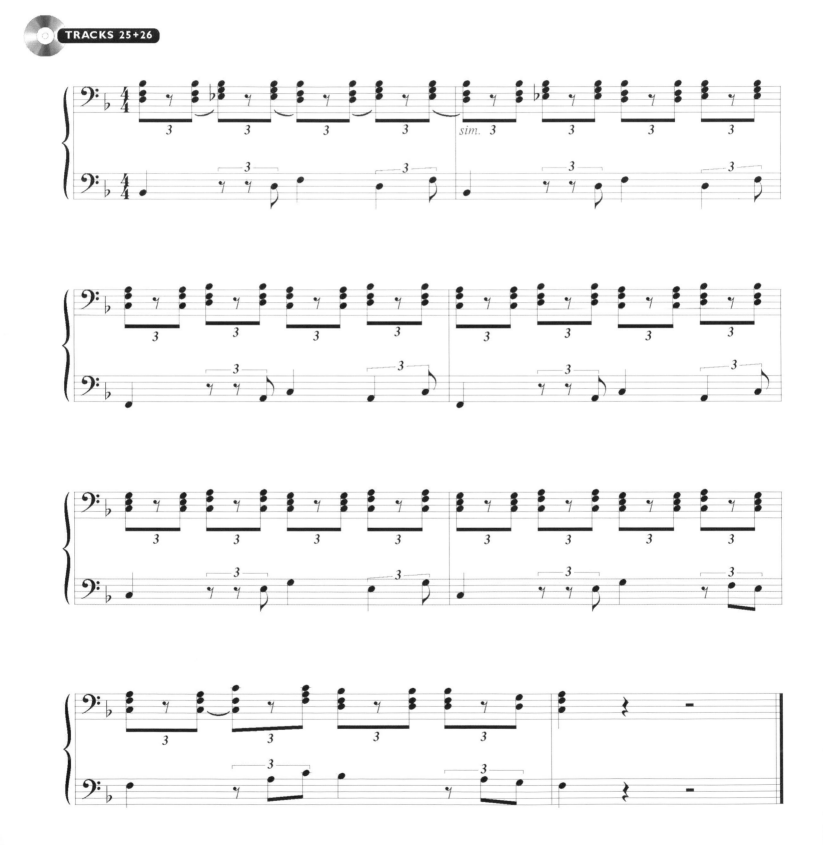

Left Right Bounce

In this example the riff is shared equally between the two hands and utilises a more open harmonic voicing. This should have a slightly languid quality so, again, you'll need to keep both wrists loose and relaxed.

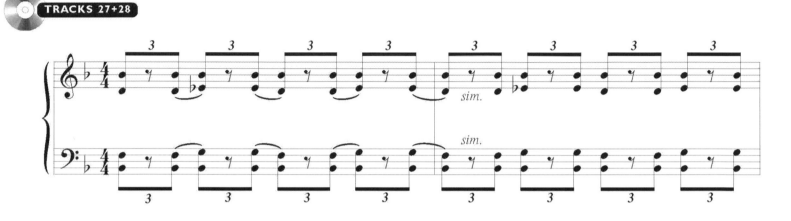

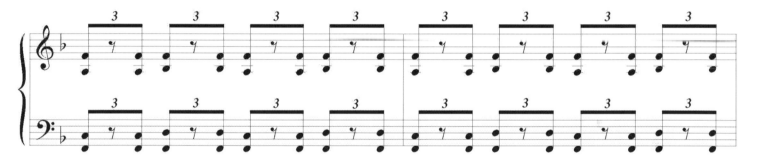

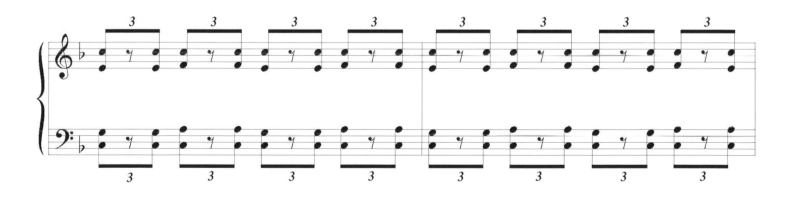

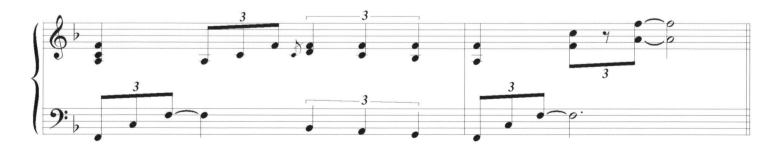

Left Hand Bounce

You may well be thinking it's a waste of a good bass player to double his line, so now we're going to try the right hand riff from page 24 in the left hand. You'll most likely find this more difficult, so beware of the wrist becoming stiff. Just remember to stay loose and once you've cracked it you probably won't want to stop.

TRACKS 29+30

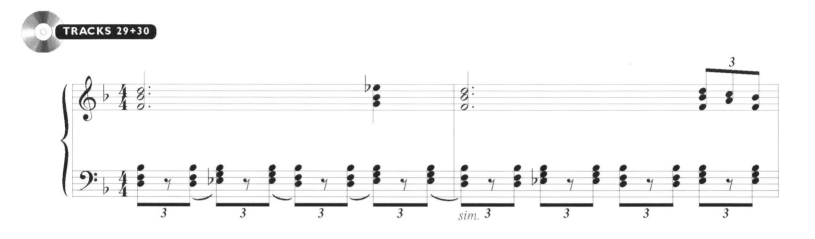

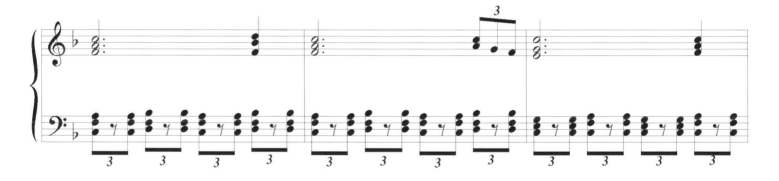

Rolling Right Bouncing Left

The major disadvantage with the piano, of course, is that as soon as you hit the note it starts to die away, so, unlike a singer, sax or trumpet, we pianists aren't able to make the notes 'grow' after sounding. There is, however, one device we can use to create the illusion of sustain or growth and that is the roll or tremolando. It's unlikely to surprise you that, what with the racket cooked up by the rest of the band and the accompanying noise of the audience, the tremolando features

quite heavily in a night's work. Although I've used the chordal riff for the left hand, you could also use the bass parts from the previous examples to start off with. It's not a bad idea to split the upper part into two elements, first playing the line without the tremolo and simply holding the chords at the start of each bar. Then, practise the tremolo over the bass but without the rest of the melodic line, and finally put all the parts together.

TRACKS 31+32

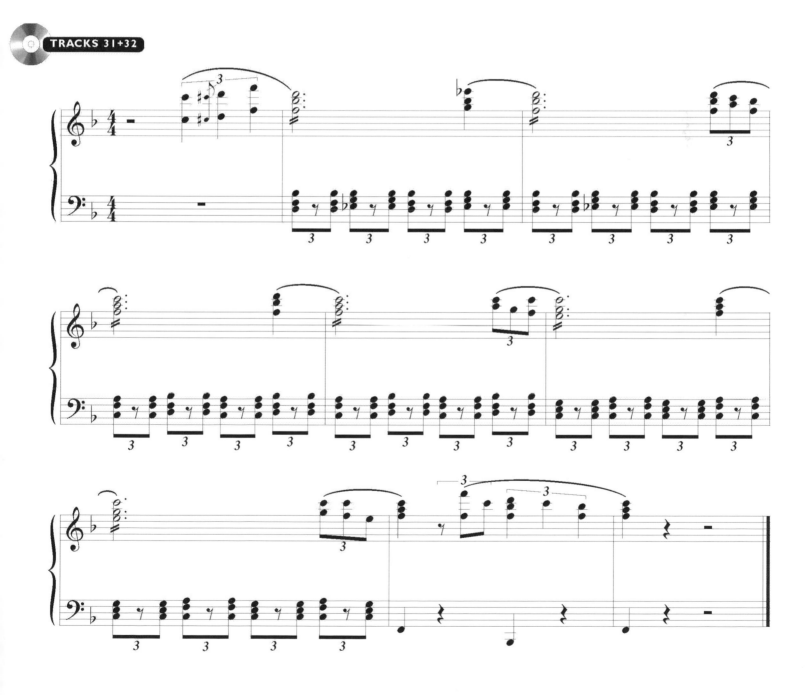

'Strawberry Pill'

Apart from the minor detail that it's some forty years late, you may well, like me, be wondering why 'Fats' never showed an interest in recording my one minute masterpiece. But now you can play a part in addressing this blatant injustice and simultaneously endear yourself to your estranged neighbours. Time to let rip!

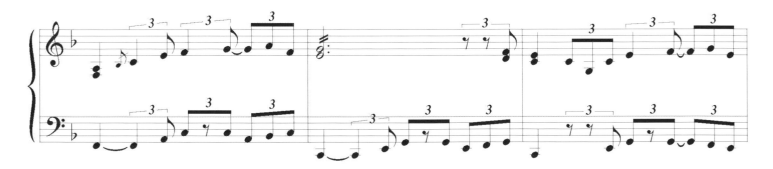

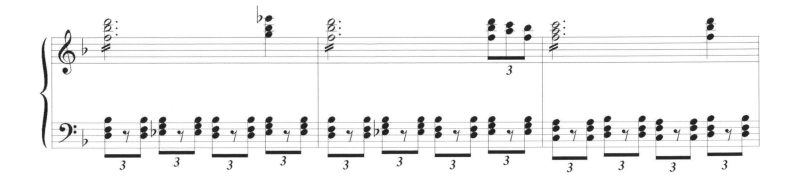

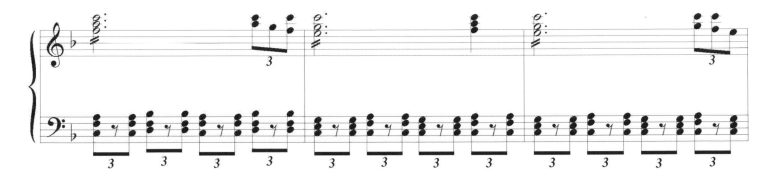

Chapter 4: Who Ray Hip Hip

The term 'genius' is used often when talking about performers, but **Ray Charles** is one of those rare individuals for whom it really is true. Coming from a background of R&B and gospel music, he was one of the pioneers of soul music and his influence on other performers was wide-ranging.

It's hard to imagine what the fuss was all about now, but his 'I got a Woman' and **Little Richard**'s 'Long Tall Sally', were banned by some southern radio stations, such was the paranoia about this 'nefarious and satanic influence of Rock 'n' Roll'. He was so versatile that choosing a single style to look at is difficult. This offering owes a debt to his 'Hallelujah I Love Her So' but is in a slower, more mid tempo groove.

▶▶ *HOWLIN' WOLF*

A Ray Of Light

In this example, the introduction is split alternately between the organ and piano. Then, the piano continues with an accompanied figure that is part harmonic and part melodic. The first of each pair of bars simply states the harmony and the second of each adds some melodic interest, dovetailing with the main tune and producing a balanced, rounded pattern.

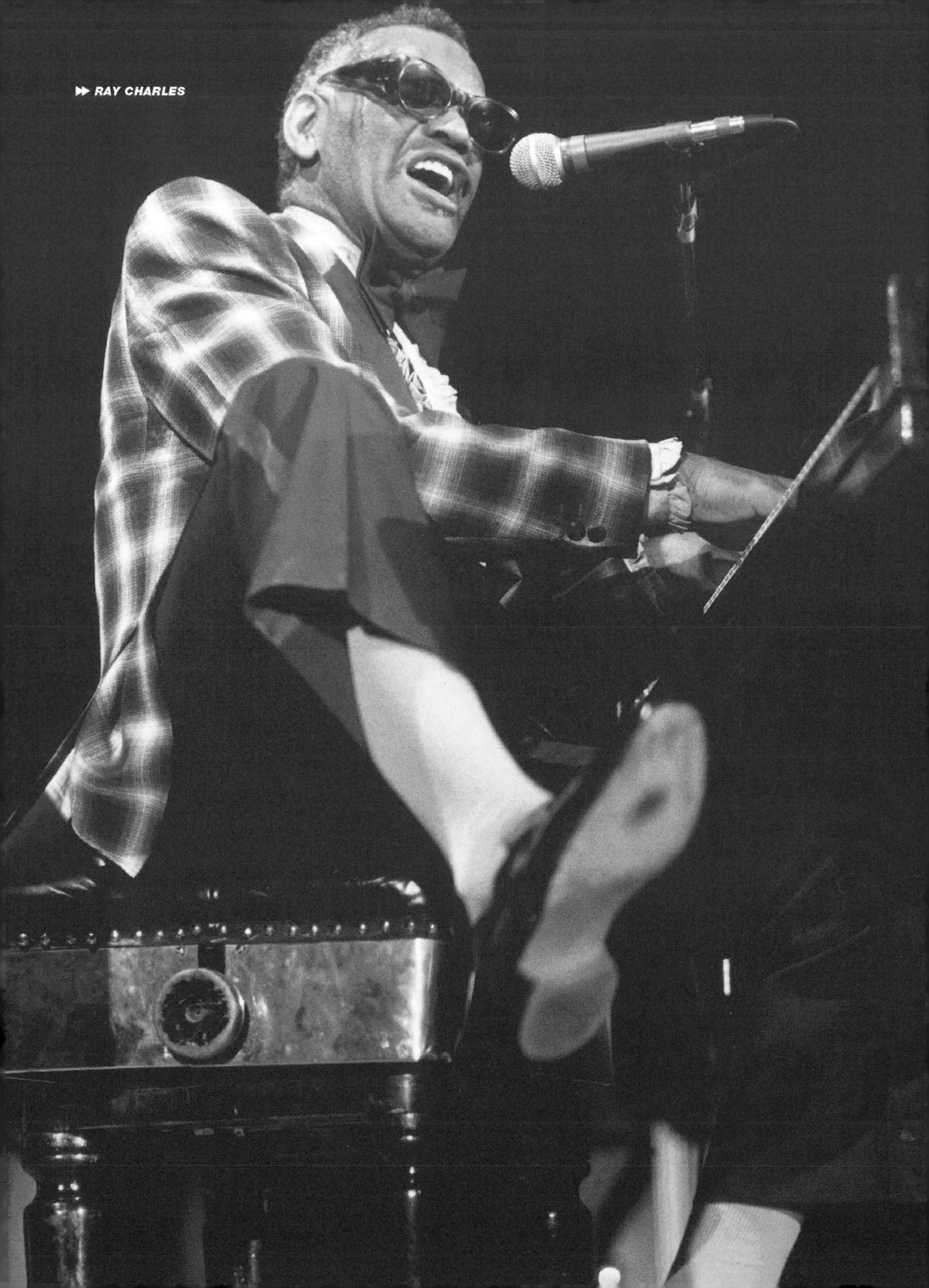

►►FastForward™
Guide To Keyboard

All You Need To Know to get you started!

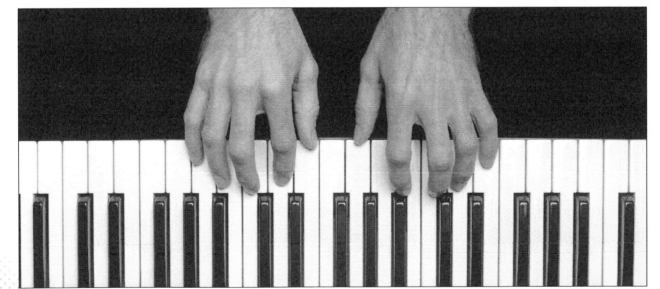

Sitting Correctly

It is important to sit correctly at the keyboard. The more comfortable you are, the easier it is to play.

Sit facing the middle of the instrument, with your feet opposite the pedals. Sit upright with as straight a back as possible without being stiff. Your seat should be high enough to allow your arms to be level with the keyboard, or slightly sloping down towards it.

The Hand Position

Support your hands from the wrists, which should be in a flat position. If you bend your wrists too much as you play, you will soon experience muscle fatigue.

Curve your fingers slightly as if you are gently holding an imaginary ball. Don't extend your fingers into the keyboard; allow the natural position of your hand to determine which part of the key you depress with the tip of your finger.

The Five Finger Playing Position

With the tips of your fingers, cover five adjacent white notes in each hand. This is the normal five finger playing position. It is also the hand's most relaxed state.

Always return to this position when you have been playing on other parts of the keyboard. Like a good squash or tennis player always occupying the centre of the court, this is the best 'alert' position for keyboard players.

How To Work Out Chords

With this easy-to-use guide you will be able to work out any major, minor, augmented and diminished chord on any note. Follow the simple formulae and all the chords you need will be at your fingertips.

Types of Chord

Broadly speaking, there are four types of chord:

MAJOR (e.g. C)
MINOR (e.g. Cm)
DIMINISHED (e.g. C°)
AUGMENTED (e.g. C+)

MAJOR and MINOR are the two most important types: popular Western music is based on them. It is possible to play most popular tunes using MAJOR and MINOR chords only.

DIMINISHED and AUGMENTED are merely 'passing' or linking chords: they are used for passing from one Major or Minor chord to another.

Working Out Your Own Chords:
Using Semitones

It is possible to work out any of the four types of chord by using simple formulae. These formulae rely on SEMITONES.

A SEMITONE is the smallest possible distance on a keyboard, counting black and white notes:-

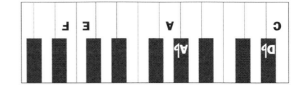

C to D♭ (or back) is the distance of
ONE SEMITONE
A♭ to A (or back) is the distance of
ONE SEMITONE
E to F (or back) is the distance of
ONE SEMITONE

Chord Formulae

MAJOR 4-3 Semitones
MINOR 3-4 Semitones
DIMINISHED 3-3 Semitones
AUGMENTED 4-4 Semitones

Example 1

To find the chord of C (Major).
Formula: C-4-3

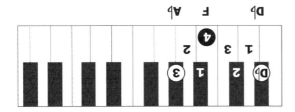

Play note C, then count 4 SEMITONES to the right, and you will arrive at the note E. Play note E, then count 3 SEMITONES to the right, and you will arrive at the note G. The notes of the chord are therefore: C, E, G.

Example 2

To find the chord of D♭ (Major).
Formula: D♭-4-3

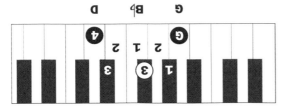

Play note D♭, then count 4 SEMITONES to the right, and you will arrive at the note F. Play note F, then count 3 SEMITONES to the right, and you will arrive at the note A♭. The notes of the chord are therefore: D♭, F, A♭.

Example 3

To find the chord of G (Minor).
Formula: G-3-4

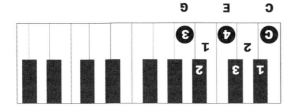

Play note G, then count 3 SEMITONES to the right, and you will arrive at the note B♭. Play note B♭, then count 4 SEMITONES to the right, and you will arrive at the note D. The notes of the chord are therefore: G, B♭, D.

Triplet Approach

This starts with an arpeggiated triplet figure, which gives it a light rhythmic impetus towards bar 3, where the previous solo pick-up takes over.

Then, under the tune, we have a semi-arpeggiated rocking figure, which provides a simple but effective accompaniment.

TRACKS 37+38

Gospel Boogie

If I had written a full-length piece, this would be one contender for the middle 8, as it uses that old favourite of pianists (and particularly guitarists) for the left-hand part. Above it we have another simple, understated melodic/harmonic mixture. The end illustrates a

syncopated figure that is neatly split between the two hands and then rhythmically displaced in the final bar. You should experiment further with this idea and others of your own invention, cycling around a sequence and starting your riff on different beats of the bar.

Hall E Lu

The right hand part in this example is similar to that on page 31, 'A Ray Of Light', in that there is a bar of primarily harmonic function, followed by a more melodic one. In the first bar I'm using a variant of the previous example's left hand figure to provide a Boogie element after which we have the melodic figuration. You will notice that the rhythmic device for the left hand, (that slots in with the right for the Boogie pattern), is the one which I used for the end of the previous example. This syncopated riff has a slightly funky element to the part.

TRACKS 41+42

Lu Jah

For this final piece the piano takes the tune for the entire introduction underpinned by a rolling bass. Thereafter the piano continues with this relaxed lazy tune, but watch out for embellishments at the start of bars 10 and 12. To extend this piece there's a repeat between bars 5 – 12, but, as before, try and come up with some variations of your own.

TRACKS 43+44

Chapter 5: Finger Lickin' Country Sound

Although he came from a country background, **Floyd Cramer**'s talent and creativity made him the chosen pianist of **Elvis Presley** and **Roy Orbison** on many recordings. His ideas are still valid and very much in use today.

One of the most important of these is the grace note or 'crushed' note (so called because it's literally crushed into the chord or adjacent notes). It's very common in Boogie-Woogie and Rock 'n' Roll. Have a look at the example below to sharpen up your crushed notes.

The other example below gives you a chance to practise your 16th-note triplets. These are another very important and commonly-used feature of Rock 'n' Roll piano.

Crushed Notes Practice

16th Note Triplets Practice

Nice 'n' Simple

We start with a simple left-right 'um-pah'
rhythm (yes, it can work in Rock 'n' Roll too).
There are no tricky syncopations to deal with, so
you should master this quite quickly, but as you
can hear from the CD it fits in nicely with
everyone else, providing an essential foundation.
For melodic interest I've added an organ part
which uses the crushed notes we'll be looking at
in a moment.

TRACKS 45+46

A Little More Bass

This keeps the right hand part you've just learnt
but gives you a little more to do with the left
hand. If you've been listening to the band you'll
have noticed that the bass guitar was playing
the same line on page 38. This illustrates an
important point regarding how much you can,
or should, duplicate. So try and be aware of the
differences in texture when you're doubling all
of the line or just some of it.

TRACKS 47+48

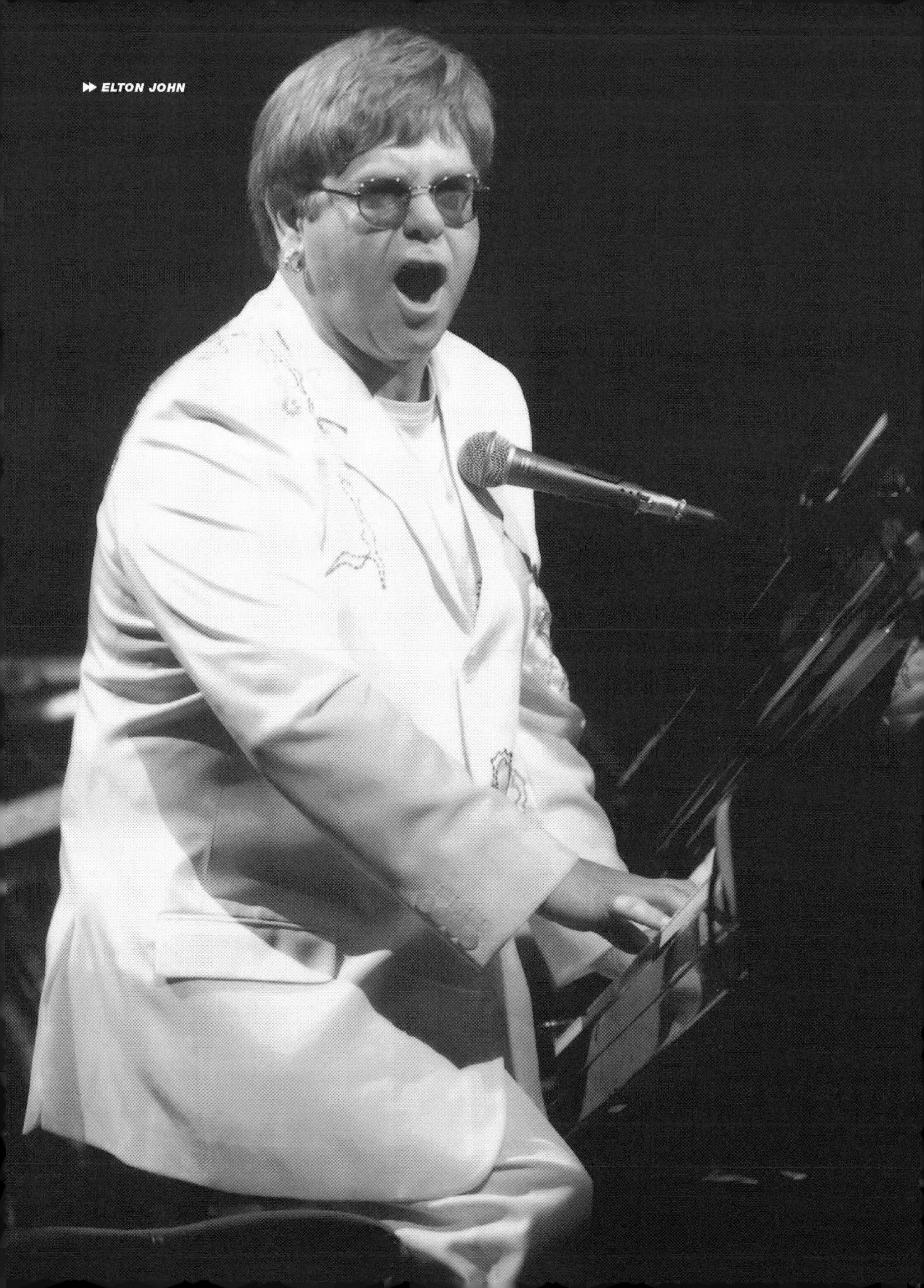

Country Crush

Now I've added the crushed notes I've been talking about, which really add some character to the piece. If your left hand's not quite secure yet or you just want to take it easy, try using the left hand part from ex.1 whilst getting your crushed notes together.

Another subtle variation in the left hand is achieved by playing the line 'legato', or smoothly, so in bars 1, 3 and 5 the bass doesn't stop on beats 2 and 4 as in the example before.

That option of pulling your left hand off the keys as you hear the crack of the snare gives the back beat a bit more space and impact. This becomes more important the more people you have in your band and it's certainly something to bear in mind when playing in a messy acoustic or your next cathedral rock gig!

TRACKS 49+50

A Touch Of Floyd

That's enough accompaniment – now it's time to
take a solo! We're still using the same harmonies
as before, but the right hand's now getting a bit
more melodic. If you're playing with a friend, you
could get them to play just the um-pah, i.e. beats
1, 2, 3, and 4 (so leave out the 8th notes) from
page 38 while you practise your right
hand an octave higher.

TRACKS 51+52

F.C. Unwound

Floyd Cramer was one of the few musicians to successfully write hit songs featuring piano without vocals, and this tune uses some of his hallmark figures which still have plenty of life. On a technical point, you might want to practise the triplet figure in isolation until it's really comfortable.

Truly Finger Lickin' Kickin' Country Sound

Now let's join together the last two examples to form a piece that would surely have Floyd quaking in his boots and probably get me my first No. 1 (hmm, back to reality!). So far in this chapter, all the grace notes have been of the diatonic variety, i.e. notes within the key, and in this piece, there are two examples of diatonic grace-notes. But, if you want to get a real 'finger lickin' Blues' sound, try substituting some white notes with black ones!

TRACKS 55+56

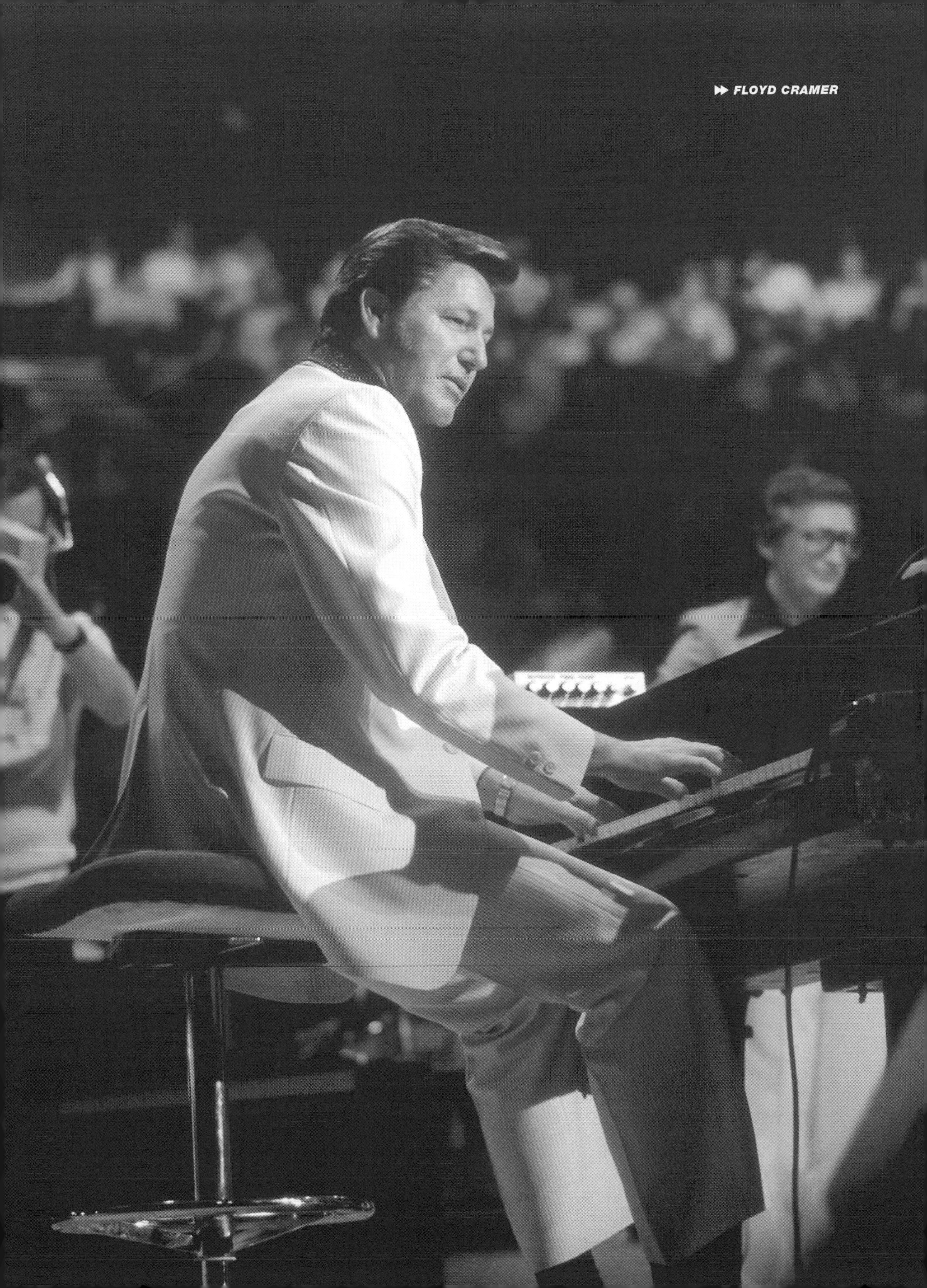

Chapter 6: Big Deal

Richard Penniman, a.k.a. **Little Richard**, had enormous energy in his playing, and if you listen to the live version of 'Lucille', the riff is laid down by the band while Richard gets stuck into the poor Joanna with more intensity than a pneumatic drill! This contrasts oddly with the tame opening in the studio version, but basically if you can hammer out continuous 8th notes for a couple of minutes your piano playing won't be lagging too far behind his.

▶▶ *LITTLE RICHARD*

The Riff

Given the shameless addiction of Rock 'n' Roll musicians to flattened 7ths and 3rds, both of which are essential notes in defining the minor scale, you could be forgiven for thinking Rock 'n' Roll tunes are predominantly in minor keys – but you'd be wrong! The appearance of the minor 3rd of the scale in a major key is usually melodic or as a 'blue note', invariably, as in this piece, rising to the major 3rd. As usual we're going to start off with a simplified version. I've intentionally limited it to two chords, but if you want to ease yourself in really slowly, just play the odd numbered bars and let the band take the strain.

TRACKS 57+58

▶▶ JOHN LENNON AND PAUL Mc CARTNEY

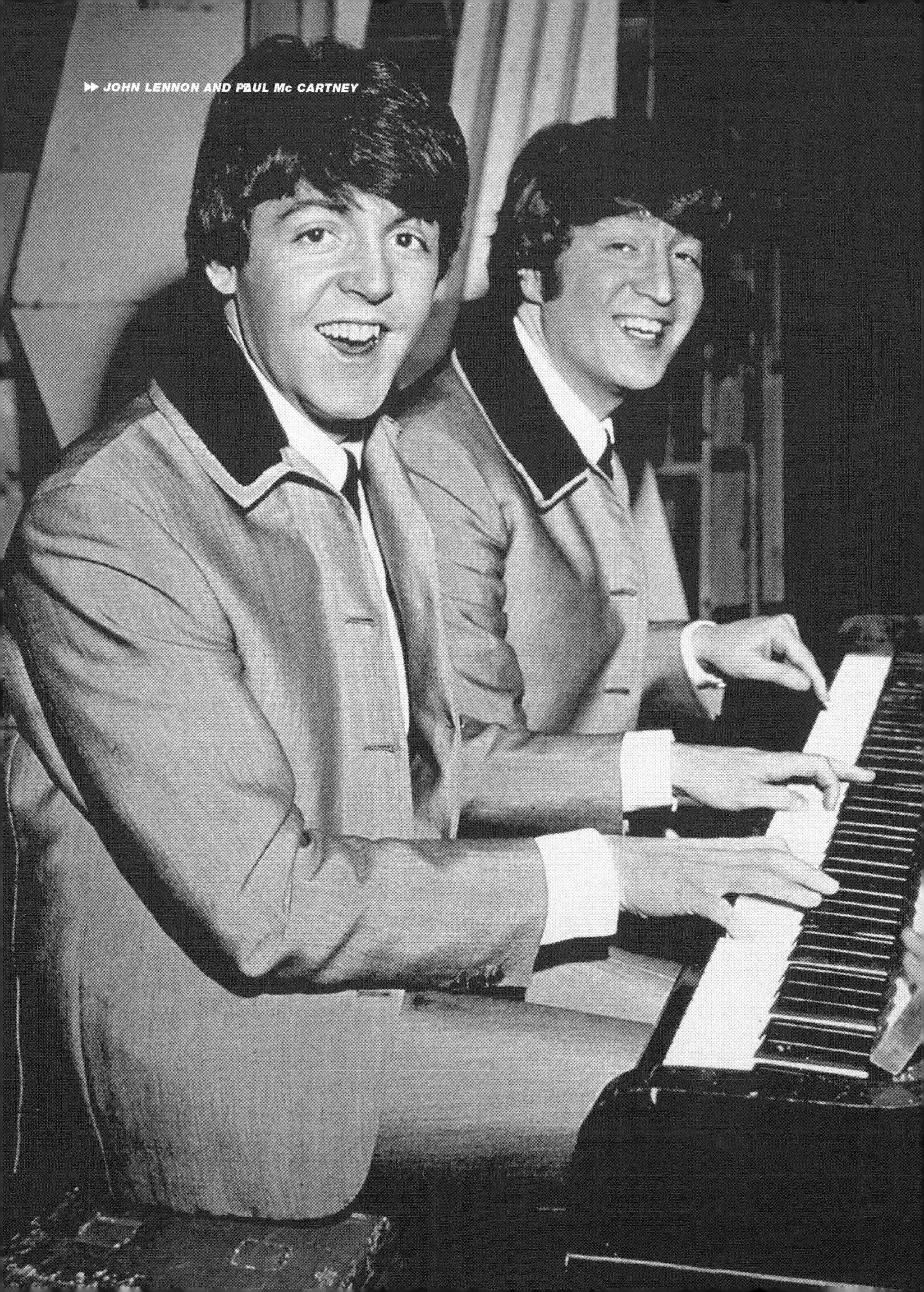

Backbeat

This would probably confirm the worst fears of your music teacher, so keep this page carefully covered, because in the true Rock 'n' Roll tradition it's time to get Neanderthal. Like the riff, the 'back beat' isn't an invention of Rock 'n' Roll. It may only be 2 and 4 but it's vital to stay in time. Listen to the drums and try and 'lock in' with the timing.

Harmony

In this example I've added some harmony to the riff in certain places, which can give it a real change of character. As you'll see it's a simple device but can be useful in adding interest when you have numerous repeats, or in defining sections (e.g. adding to the chorus). It will normally be a 3rd or 6th that will work best but beware, as it can sound really tortuous if you try to do the whole riff. One example that works really well on the whole line is **The Beatles**' 'Money (That's What I Want)'. If you're into guitar bands and want to hear some great riff harmonisations, check out **Ted Turner** and **Andy Powell**'s great duetting in 'Wishbone Ash'.

Fills

You won't have failed to notice that every 4th bar has been empty so far. The intention here has been to give you some time to get the main riff secure and hopefully emphasise the difference between the two sections:- the riff, and the fill. But now, apart from the drums keeping time, the rest of the band will drop out to give you a chance to shine. Why not try the fills by themselves, before adding the riff. Apart from making it easier of course, this should also help you to respond to the two different sections; e.g. attacking the fills a bit more, or introducing your own rhythmic subtleties or variations when you're not having to phrase in unison with the band.

TRACKS 63+64

Chuck And Jerry

The opening break of this next example owes more than a nod to **Chuck Berry**'s flamboyant style. Although Chuck was a guitarist, his influence in the late 1950s was huge on all musicians and still lasts today.

In bars 6 and 7 we encounter another classic Rock 'n' Roll figure. Like numerous other Rock 'n' Roll ideas this is based on the simple but enduringly effective pattern of grouping in threes. In an effort to illustrate this visually I've grouped these bars in a slightly unusual way which I hope you'll find helpful. To finish we have a fleeting but timeless offering from another Rock 'n' Roll legend, **Jerry Lee Lewis**. Have a listen to Jerry Lee's 'Dancing At The High School Hop', or, to hear those descending triplets really sparkle, there are no better examples than **Keith Emerson**'s wizardry with **E.L.P**.

▶▶ *KEITH EMERSON*

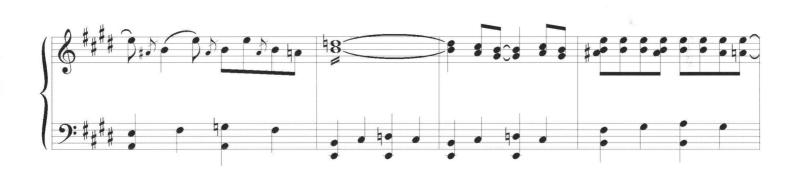

The Full Monty

The final example of this chapter begins with
'Chuck and Jerry' and then moves on to more
harmonic (chordal) playing. It's a little longer
than previous examples, to give you something to
get stuck in to.

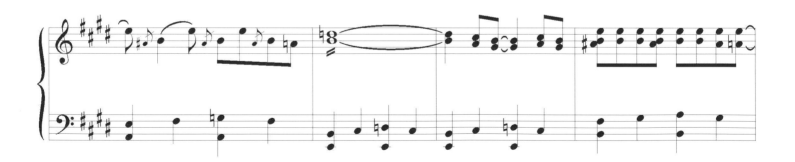

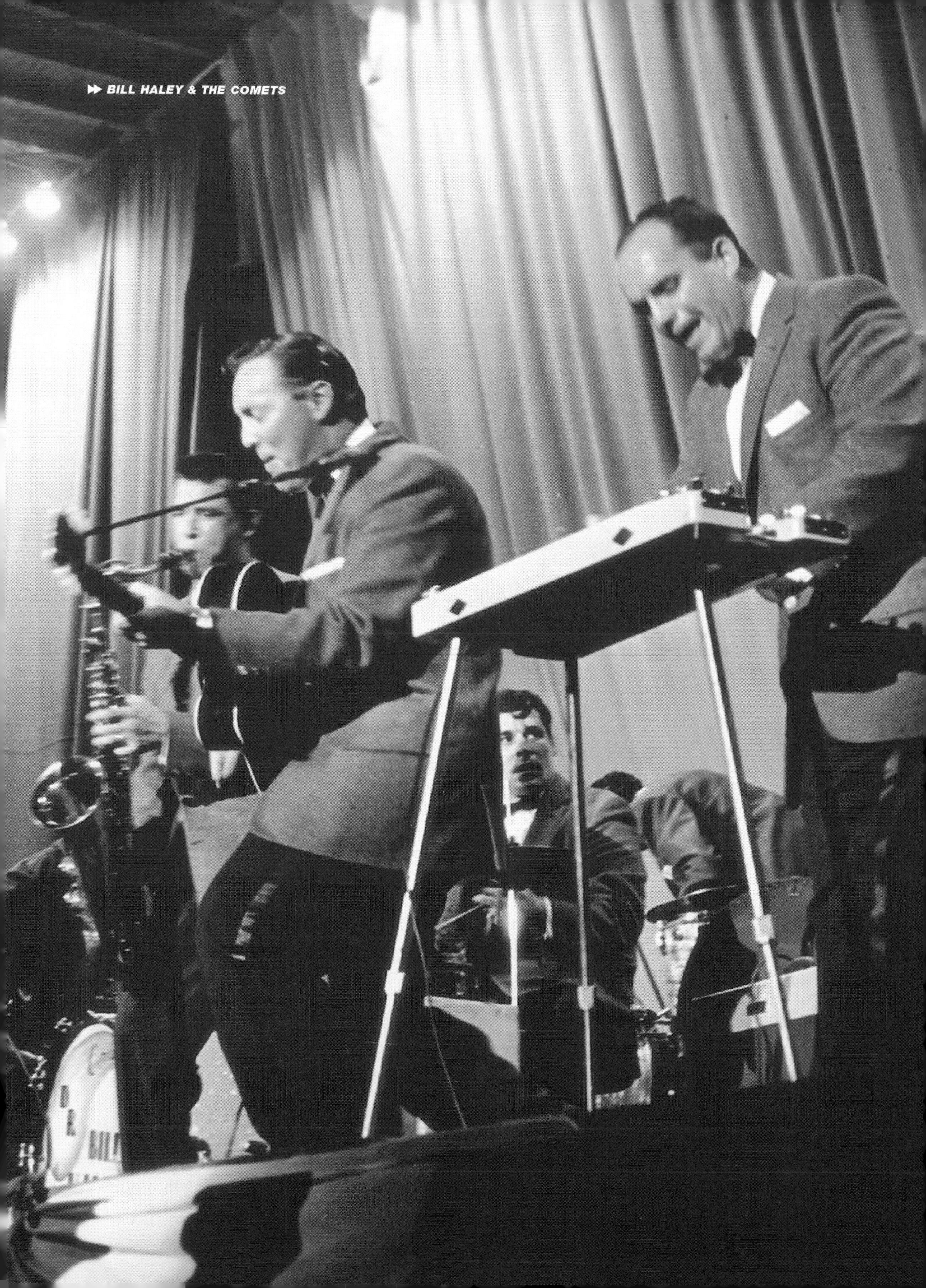

Chapter 7: Solitaire

Brass Stab

This left hand bass line pattern is one of the most enduring in popular music. Frequently appearing in several musical styles from the big bands of more than a decade earlier to present day country-swing, that 1-3-5-6 arpeggio unobtrusively defines the harmony and pushes the band dynamically on. The right hand part starts with an equally classic big band brass figure with a simple syncopation that complements the left hand perfectly.

TRACKS 69+70

Walking Bass Basic Tune

Here I've kept the walking bass and added a simple tune above it. This illustrates an approach to improvising and how much mileage you can get out of four notes – C G A and B♭, which makes up the main melodic material of the first eight bars. Try creating a three or four note melody of your own, and then see how many variations you can come up with.

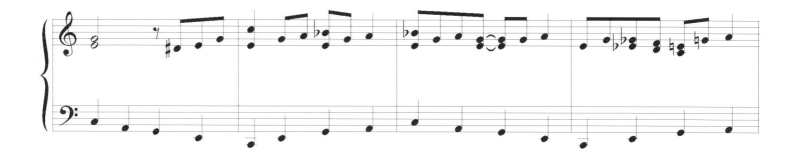

Easy Right Broken Left

This time the left hand part has something new for you to work on. It's a simplified version of a timeless boogie bass pattern and is something you'll really need to nail if you're serious about Rock 'n' Roll piano. As always you should get each hand down before putting them together but the right hand shouldn't take too much work this time.

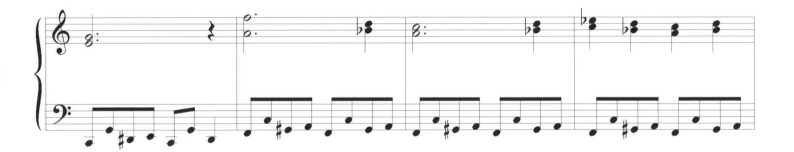

Basic Right Broken Bass

Here, the right hand introduces some further, slightly more difficult embellishments to those on page 59. The tough bit is adding the two hands together.

The left hand demonstrates some further variations, but don't feel you have to stick to them. If one variant feels more comfortable than the others, then just mix and match as you go!

TRACKS 75+76

Break Star

So far in this book, I've notated the music in even quavers, which should be played in a bounced or swung rhythm (i.e. broken triplets). Another way to notate this same rhythm is as a dotted quaver/semi-quaver pattern. I've written

the last two pieces this way as it's useful to become accustomed to reading it either way. Just remember, it should be played the same as before, despite its different appearance.

TRACKS 77+78

Time To Swear

Blaspheming? Well I'd be surprised if you aren't swearing now, as this is really quite difficult. Once you've cracked it, you'll probably be glued to your piano stool all night!

There are numerous examples of boogie piano used in Rock 'n' Roll tunes without changing a note and it's fair to say it's the biggest single influence on Rock 'n' Roll piano. Why not take a look at *Fastforward Boogie Woogie Piano* if you're interested in this?

Several **Elvis** hits feature this style – for example, 'All Shook Up', or 'Let's Have A Party'.

Whether or not you're an **Elvis** fan you should really get hold of 'Teddy Bear' for the stonking piano playing of **Dudley Brooks**.

TRACKS 79+80

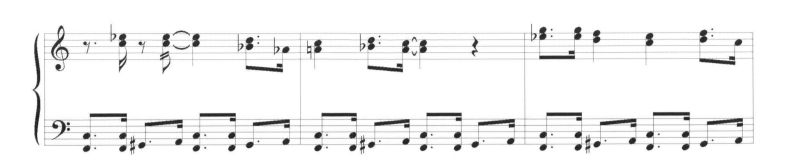

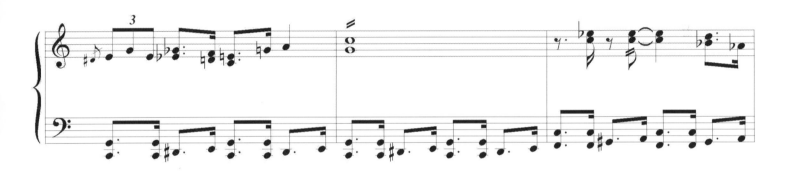

Further Reading

Congratulations – it's time to book some gigs! I hope you've learnt something and, more importantly, had fun doing it. As I said before, you should never just stick to what's in front of you – play what you can, and simplify what you can't. Here's hoping I see you at No.1 soon!

If you'd like to continue improving your piano or keyboard playing, why not check out some of these great books, available from all good music retailers or bookshops.

Chord Encyclopaedias

The essential source books for all piano and keyboard players. 384 blues chords and 480 jazz chords in standard notation, plus keyboard diagrams, for instant note recognition.

**The Encyclopaedia Of
Blues Chords** AM92592

**The Encyclopaedia Of
Jazz Chords** AM92591

FastForward 12-Bar Blues Piano
AM92445

Discover the blues with this book and CD pack. Includes basic blues structures and techniques, original blues to jazz and rock piano, boogie, stride and walking bass styles.

FastForward Boogie-Woogie Piano
AM958925

Learn this infectious 'foot-stomping' piano style and create the boogie sounds of great pianists such as Jools Holland, Jelly Roll Morton and Professor Longhair.

FastForward Real Blues For Keyboard
AM92438

Learn to play the 12-bar blues using authentic techniques, to get the real blues sound. Play along with the CD, and discover how bands get their sound.